19 Rhinoceros · 20 Sloth · 21 Snow leopard · 22 Red deer · 23 Horse · 24 Bear · 25 Moufflon · 26 Buffalo
27 Camel · 28 Rat · 29 Giraffe · 30 Bison · 31 Llama · 32 Elk · 33 Chamois · 34 Leopard · 35 Puma · 36 Tortoise

The African Elephant

The elephant is the world's largest land *mammal*. This enormous animal lives on the African savannah, which is a huge grassy plain where few trees grow.

The elephant loves to eat plants and leaves, especially the highest and most tender branches of the *acacia* tree.

The elephant can do everything with its trunk – it can use it to uproot a tree, fight a rival, or simply drink and give itself a shower.

Published in the UK in 1994 by
Schofield & Sims Limited, Huddersfield, England.

0 7217 5006 0

FIRST IMPRESSIONS

Wild Animals

Schofield & Sims Limited Huddersfield.

Some Wild Animals

1 Antelope · 2 Tiger · 3 Zebra · 4 Hippopotamus · 5 Stag · 6 Hare · 7 Wild boar · 8 Wolf · 9 Squirrel · 10 Elephant
11 Cheetah · 12 Hyena · 13 Koala Bear · 14 Kangaroo · 15 Hedgehog · 16 Fox · 17 Roe deer · 18 Red panda

In the elephant family, the grandmother guides the youngsters and passes on her knowledge to them.

At birth, a baby elephant weighs about 100 kilograms – the weight of 30 human babies!

The Lion

The lion owes his title 'King of Beasts' to his magnificent mane, his majestic bearing, and his terrifying roars.

The lion is the only cat that lives in a group, called a pride.

It is the lionesses who hunt to feed the family.

The Tiger

The tiger lives in the jungles of Asia and is the largest cat in the world. A tiger always has a stream or river in its territory because tigers love the coolness of water. They are very strong swimmers.

The tiger hunts large animals, as well as tortoises, birds, and even *locusts*.

The dark stripes of a tiger's coat are a perfect camouflage amidst the tall grass and in the forest.

The Polar Bear

The polar bear is the largest *carnivore* on Earth.

It is an excellent swimmer and can swim for over 100 kilometres without stopping!

With its well-developed sense of smell, the polar bear can locate a seal over 30 kilometres away.

The polar bear lives alone on the ice-floe, an icy desert around the North Pole.

The female bear digs out a cave in the frozen snow where she gives birth to her cubs.

Because of their white fur, the cubs cannot easily be seen on the ice-floe.

The Kangaroo

The kangaroo and the koala bear live in Australia.
They are both marsupials – they have a pouch on their stomach.
After baby kangaroos are born, they live in the pouch for several months to give them time to grow.

The kangaroo is a jumping champion – it can high-jump over 3 metres and long-jump over 9 metres!

While in its mother's pouch, the baby kangaroo is completely naked. It weighs only 1 gram and measures less than 5 cm at birth.

The Koala Bear

On the ground, the koala bear is very clumsy. It only really feels at home in the trees and is an excellent climber.

The koala eats only the leaves of the eucalyptus tree, which provide it with the water it needs.

Desert Animals

Camels can have one hump or two humps. A camel with one hump is often called a dromedary.

The camel's hump is a kind of food store from which the animal takes water and nourishment when it needs them.

In the desert, days are hot, nights are cold, and water is scarce. However, many animals have adapted to live in these difficult conditions. They have learned how to protect themselves from the sun and wind, and how to survive on very little water.

The fennec is a desert fox. The hair under its paws allows it to walk over the sand-dunes without sinking.

Some gazelles live in desert regions. A gazelle can run very quickly – often as fast as 70 kilometres an hour.

The Chimpanzee

The chimpanzee and the gorilla of Africa are the animals which look most like humans. Their hands have five fingers, as ours have. They have learned how to use simple tools.

When it isn't feasting on fruit, the chimpanzee uses a blade of grass to help it to reach its favourite food – ants.

Chimpanzees love being together – being alone makes them very miserable.

The Gorilla

Like us, the gorilla sleeps about ten hours at night. It also has a nap in the afternoon.

Baby gorillas are very playful and mischievous, but the older gorillas are very patient and do not mind when they play tricks.

The Wolf

For centuries, people have been afraid of the wolf. However, it is a shy and cautious creature that lives in packs.

The male and female wolf remain faithful to each other for life.

Wolf-cubs love playing with pebbles and leaves. When they are about two months old, they start to learn how to hunt.

The Fox

The fox hunts mainly at night. Its stamina and legendary cunning help it to survive in the worst conditions.

The rabbit is the fox's favourite food. But it also eats eggs, earthworms, fruit and *cereals* when it can.

The fox raises its young in a burrow. This also serves as a shelter when it rains or when danger threatens.

The Cheetah

The graceful cheetah is the fastest *mammal* in the world. When it chases gazelles on the African savannah, its speed can reach over 100 kilometres an hour.

Cheetah cubs purr while they are suckling. When they are small, their mother carries them everywhere in her jaws.

The cheetah has two black lines running from the corner of its eye and along the length of its *muzzle*. These 'tear marks' make the cheetah look rather sad.

The Jaguar

The jaguar lives in the forests of South America. To catch its prey, it lies in wait and keeps very still. A jaguar can kill animals much bigger than itself.

The jaguar is very good at catching fish.

It particularly likes to eat tortoises or *terrapins*.

The Giant Panda

This solitary animal lives in the mountains of China and has become a symbol of *conservation*. Giant pandas are rare – there are only about 1000 left in the world.

The panda spends over 10 hours a day eating. It eats mainly bamboo shoots, although sometimes it eats fruit and fish as well as small animals. It often eats sitting upright with its legs stretched out.

The panda is an excellent climber. It comes down the tree backwards.

The panda's black and white fur helps it to hide in the undergrowth among the bamboo plants. Its thick fur also protects it from cold and rain.

A baby panda does not walk until it is three or four months old. When the mother leaves her shelter, she carries her baby with her.

The Beaver

The clever beaver is a lumberjack, an architect and a builder. Above all, the beaver is an *aquatic* animal which builds dams across rivers and constructs shelters, called lodges, for its family.

The beaver gnaws through tree-trunks and then uses its sharp teeth to cut the logs into shorter pieces of wood.

The beaver travels about like a boat – its paws act as oars and its tail acts like a *rudder*.

A beaver family is very close. The little ones grow up with their older sisters and brothers.

The beaver always keeps the inside of its lodge tidy, and frequently changes the wood-shavings that cover the floor of its home.

The Rhinoceros

The rhinoceros is easily recognised by its enormous horn. It lives on the edge of the forest and the savannah. Because it has very poor eyesight, the rhinoceros finds its way around by using its sense of smell – one of the best in the animal kingdom.

The rhinoceros is a *herbivore*. Its thick hide protects it from the thorny bushes on the savannah.

The tick-bird keeps the skin of the rhinoceros clean and warns the animal of danger.

The Hippopotamus

Although the hippopotamus is a land animal, it spends most of its life dozing in calm, muddy water.

By closing their nostrils and ears, hippopotamuses are able to walk around under the water for several minutes without breathing.

When the sun goes down, the hippopotamus comes out of the water to graze.

Glossary

Acacia

A tree with yellow or white flowers, very common on the African savannah.

Aquatic

Growing or living in or near water.

Carnivore

An animal that eats the flesh of other creatures.

Cereals

Crops that are cultivated for their grains, such as wheat, oats, barley, maize or rice.

Conservation

Protecting the environment, especially the countryside and animal life.

Herbivore

An animal that eats grass and plants, but not meat.

Locust

A type of grasshopper that likes dry and sunny places.

Mammal

An animal which feeds its young with its own milk. The elephant and the cheetah are mammals – so are humans.

Muzzle

The part of an animal's face that includes the nose and mouth.

Rudder

A piece of wood or metal fixed at the back of a boat to steer it.

Terrapin

A type of small freshwater turtle.